I0155365

THE
LORD'S
PRAYER

A Contemplative Journey Through Sacred Words

Gilda Wray
Wray of Light Publishing
2025

THE LORD'S PRAYER
A Contemplative Journey Through Sacred Words

Gilda Wray

WRAY OF LIGHT
PUBLISHING

In memory of my father,
who taught me to look—and to see.
I am still finding treasure.

Published by Wray of Light Publishing
Lacey, WA, USA

Email: gildawray@tuta.com

Scripture quotations are taken from the Septuagint (LXX) and the Greek New Testament where noted, adapted by the author for clarity and poetic flow.

First Edition

ISBN: 978-1-968631-01-7

Table of Contents

About the Author

Gilda Wray's father teased that her first word was "why"—a curiosity that has shaped her lifetime exploration of faith and language. Working directly from Greek texts, she seeks to understand how Jesus's first audiences would have heard His teachings, imagining not just the words but the full sensory reality of Scripture. This contemplative approach led to the groundbreaking discoveries in this book, particularly her analysis of the mysterious word ἐπιούσιον (epiousion) found nowhere else in ancient literature. Through Wray of Light Publishing, she continues exploring how ancient words can spring to new life.

Prologue

Come in. The fire's still warm. You can hear it crackle, even if you don't see the flame yet. You can smell the faint scent of woodsmoke and something ancient in the air. There's a chair here for you. A place prepared. And a quiet voice, familiar and strong, whispers,

Come and see. This is for you.

You may not feel ready. That's okay. This is not the kind of table where readiness matters. Only hunger. Only wonder. Only the willingness to sit and listen, even if your hands still tremble.

This is not a book of information. It is a room—a sacred space where firelight meets breath, and where the One who spoke stars into being waits to speak again—this time, into you.

So settle in. Let the warmth rise. Let the noise fall away.

The prayer you've prayed a thousand times is about to become a place you've never been. Not a ritual. Not a rhythm. A reality.

He is here. And He has something to say.

When you pray, say…

And the fire flickers.

And the silence listens.

And the words begin to walk.

The Way of Prayer

Jesus didn't say "pray these words."
He said "pray in this way" (οὕτως προσεύχεσθε - houtōs proseuchesthe).

The distinction matters profoundly.
One offers a formula; the other reveals a framework.
One provides a script; the other opens a path.

What follows is not merely a sequence of petitions,
but the very architecture of transformation—
a way of aligning ourselves with the movement of God,
of participating in what He is already doing,
of becoming dwelling places for His presence.

Introduction

This book began as a question: What if the prayer we've prayed a thousand times could become a place we've never been?

What if these familiar words—worn smooth by repetition—still held fire waiting to be kindled? What if Jesus wasn't just giving us something to say, but a way to be transformed?

Words are meant to meet with Spirit and spring to Life. This is the sacred alchemy Scripture invites—not dead letters on ancient pages, but living encounter with the Living Word. When the Logos breathes through language, prayer becomes presence, recitation becomes relationship, and familiar phrases reveal depths we never imagined.

God has always revealed Himself as fire—dynamic, alive, drawing us near while calling us to reverence. Fire that moves and breathes, contains all colors, transforms everything it touches.

The pages that follow are written for those who hunger for this depth—who sense that beneath familiar words lies unfamiliar territory, waiting to be explored.

This is contemplative reading. It asks not just for your mind, but for your heart, your breath, your willingness to approach the holy ground where words burn with presence—like Moses before the bush that blazed but was not consumed.

The fire is still burning.
And it has something to say.

CHAPTER ONE

Our Father in the Heavens

Πάτερ ἡμῶν ὁ ἐν τοῖς οὐρανοῖς (Pater hēmōn ho en tois ouranois)

Before anything is asked, before the needs or the fears or the failings find their voice, there is this:

Our Father in the heavens...

It is the first breath of belonging. The first truth spoken aloud: we are not alone. We are not abandoned. We are not without origin or care or name.

The Greek begins with Πάτερ ἡμῶν (Pater hēmōn) - "Father of us."

Not distant deity. Not ruler, tyrant, or cold judge. Father. Near. Intimate. The One who gives us being.

And not my Father only—our Father.

The prayer begins by undoing isolation. By placing us in a family. By drawing a circle wider than our own lives.

ὁ ἐν τοῖς οὐρανοῖς (ho en tois ouranois) - "The One in the heavens"

Not a location on a map, but a realm of presence and authority.

He is above, but not far. He is holy, but not hidden. He is seated in the heavens—yes—but also:

- in the burning bush,
- in the whisper,
- in the bread,
- in the breath.

To say "our Father in the heavens" is to name the One whose nearness fills all things, whose presence both humbles and heals.

The God who formed humanity from dust is the same who calls us children. The One who thunders from Sinai is the same who now invites us to say, "Abba."

This is not the preface to a prayer. This is the miracle.

It is the door that opens every other line that follows.

He is our Father. In the heavens. And right here.

And He is listening.

The Three "Let Be's"

Before the prayer asks for daily bread, before it names the debts or cries out for rescue, it opens with three divine declarations.

Three "Let be" statements.

Let Your name be hallowed.
Let Your Kingdom come.
Let Your will be done.

This is no accident. This is a holy pattern—an echo of the very beginning:

> Let there be light…

In Genesis, creation begins with words spoken into emptiness. And here, in this prayer, a new creation begins the same way.

These three lines are not requests in the ordinary sense. They are acts of alignment. They are spoken realities, offered not to persuade God, but to posture the soul.

We do not command. We consent.

We do not shape heaven by these words. We allow heaven to shape us.

They are the prayer's Decalogue of Desire: not commandments for the world, but invitations to transformation.

One for the Name. One for the Reign. One for the Will.

Each "Let be" is a spark—and where three gather, a fire is kindled.

So before the prayer comes down to earth, before it feeds and forgives and frees—it lifts our hearts to heaven.

And we find that heaven is already reaching for us.

Let there be awe. Let there be Kingdom. Let there be surrender.

Let it be so.

CHAPTER TWO

Hallowed Be Your Name

ἁγιασθήτω τὸ ὄνομά σου (hagiasthētō to onoma sou)

L et there be awe. That's what this line speaks into the soul. Not fear, not distance, but a reverent trembling—the kind that happens when light pierces shadow or when silence becomes presence.

Hallowed be Your name.

Not made holy, as though it were not before. But let it be revealed as holy—here, now, in us.

The Greek word is ἁγιασθήτω (hagiasthētō)—an aorist passive imperative.

It is a prayer not of effort, but of reception. Let it be so. Let Your name be unveiled. Let the world see You as You are.

This is Genesis language—"Let there be..." A prayer that echoes the first creation and invites the new one.

Your Name.

Not just a label. Not just a sound. But the fullness of who You are.

In the ancient world, a name held essence. To hallow the Name was to reverence the being. To say, "Let Your Name be holy," was to say:

Let the world know who You truly are.

This is a prayer of alignment. Before we ask for bread, forgiveness, rescue—we ask for vision.

That His holiness would be revealed. That the veil would lift. That His Name would burn bright through the fog.

And as we pray it, we are changed.

To hallow His Name is to become a vessel through which that holiness is made known.

It is not just reverence. It is transformation.

It is the fire that purifies, the whisper that steadies, the Name that calls us out of hiding.

Let it be so.

Let His Name be known in you.

CHAPTER THREE

Your Kingdom Come

ἐλθέτω ἡ βασιλεία σου (elthetō hē basileia sou)

The King is not far. That's what this line dares to proclaim. In the shadow of empire, in the ache of injustice, in the silence where longing waits—this line says:

> The Kingdom is near.
> Your Kingdom come.

Not just a hope. A declaration. A longing too holy to stay silent.

The Greek: ἐλθέτω ἡ βασιλεία σου (elthetō hē basileia sou) - "Let it come, the Kingdom of You."

The verb is imperative. But not commanding God—opening ourselves.

Let it come. Let it arrive here, now. Not someday, not elsewhere—here.

This is not about escape. It is about invasion—heaven touching earth, will aligning with will, space folding into presence.

To pray this is to surrender territory. To say:

Reign in me.
Reign in us.
Reign here, where we still build our own little kingdoms.

The Kingdom is not like the kingdoms of the world. It comes not with coercion, but with compassion. Not with swords, but with seeds. Not with pride, but with presence.

It is yeast in the dough, a treasure in the field, a whisper in the soul.

It is what we long for even when we don't have words.

And when we pray, "Your Kingdom come," we are not just asking. We are stepping into its coming.

We become the soil. The story. The sign.

And the King is not far. He is here.

Let it come.

CHAPTER FOUR

Your Will Be Done on Earth as in Heaven

γενηθήτω τὸ θέλημά σου, ὡς ἐν οὐρανῷ καὶ ἐπὶ γῆς
(genēthētō to thelēma sou, hōs en ouranō kai epi gēs)

This is the prayer that turns surrender into flame.

Your will be done,
on earth as it is in heaven.

Not resignation. Not giving up. But entering in.

The Greek: γενηθήτω τὸ θέλημά σου (genēthētō to thelēma sou) - "Let Your will come into being."

Let it happen. Let it take form—like light from the Word, like fruit from the seed.

This is Genesis language again. "Let there be..." And it was good.

To pray this is to say:

Align me.
Break what must be broken.
Heal what must be healed.
Speak again over my chaos,
and call it good.

It is not passivity. It is participation.

This is the will that hovered over the waters. That called Abram from Ur. That chose a manger over a throne. That walked dusty roads toward a cross.

And when Jesus prays this in Gethsemane, it costs Him everything.

> Not My will, but Yours…

He was not just teaching the will of God. He was becoming it.

So that we might walk in it—not as slaves, but as sons and daughters who know the voice of the Father.

To pray this is to say: Let heaven shape earth. Let the unseen shape the seen. Let eternity shape now.

It is a dangerous prayer, if prayed with open hands.

But it is the only one that leads to peace.

Because His will is not the crushing of ours. It is the healing of it.

And the King who calls us to pray this is the one who walked it first.

He is the Ladder between heaven and earth. He is the Way, the Truth, the Life.

Let it be done.

CHAPTER FIVE

Give Us This Day Our Daily Bread

τὸν ἄρτον ἡμῶν τὸν ἐπιούσιον δὸς ἡμῖν σήμερον
(ton arton hēmōn ton epiousion dos hēmin sēmeron)

Some prayers ask for fire. Some ask for the heavens to rend open. This one asks for bread.

And yet—this may be the boldest request of all.

Because this is the prayer of those who bring no offering but hunger, no performance but open hands.

This is the child asking with confidence: "Give."

Not just for sustenance. But for being. For what we cannot manufacture. For what only the Giver of Life can place into our hands.

What the Greek Reveals

There is a word in this prayer that no one had heard before.

It doesn't echo any other passage. It has no precedent in classical speech, no shadow in the Septuagint, no sibling in Greek philosophy. It arrives here—sudden, singular, startling.

ἐπιούσιον (epiousion)

It stops the breath like a whispered name you recognize but can't place.

It isn't the normal word for "daily." It's not a calendar term. It doesn't refer to schedule, appetite, or marketplace supply.

This word is something else.

The early Church knew it. Origen called it mysterious. Jerome translated it into Latin as supersubstantialem—above substance, beyond essence.

So we slow down. We listen.

The Core: οὐσία (ousia)

The root of the word is οὐσία (ousia)—a Greek word that means being, essence, the very core of what truly is.

To the philosophers of the ancient world, οὐσία (ousia) meant more than existence. It was what endures, what remains when all else falls away, what defines reality at its deepest level.

When the early Church spoke of the Trinity, they said the Father, Son, and Spirit share one οὐσία (ousia)—one divine essence, eternal and indivisible.

So when Jesus places this word inside the prayer, He is not simply speaking of bread that fills the stomach. He is speaking of bread that touches our essence—that nourishes our being, that draws us into union with the Source of Life.

This is the bread that sustains not just our days, but our communion with the One who is.

It is the daily outpouring of the Spirit—the essence of God, given to us like morning manna.

It is the breath of new creation, whispering again over the dust.

Just as in Genesis, when God formed humanity and breathed life into the nostrils of clay, this bread is the breath of that same Spirit, restoring what was lost, rekindling what was dormant, re-creating what has been forgotten.

This is the substance of restoration. The meal of becoming. The gift that comes not from below us, but upon us—ἐπί (epi).

Bread that descends from God's own essence and touches ours.

The Descent: ἐπί (epi)

If οὐσία (ousia) is essence, then ἐπί (epi) is what moves toward it—what rests upon and fills it.

The word ἐπί (epi) in Greek carries many meanings:

- Upon
- Above
- Toward
- Over
- In the presence of
- In continuation with

It is a directional word, but not from us toward heaven—rather, from heaven toward us.

In Scripture, ἐπί (epi) is the word used when:

- The Spirit comes upon someone (Luke 1:35; Acts 1:8)
- A blessing is spoken upon a person
- A name is written upon a forehead
- A dove descends and rests upon Jesus
- The fire rests upon each one at Pentecost

So when Jesus teaches us to pray for ἐπιούσιον (epiousion) bread, He's not only asking us to believe in a God who sustains—but a God who descends, covers, fills, dwells.

This is not just food for today. It is the Presence that rests upon us, like glory upon the tabernacle, like breath upon the clay, like fire upon the heads of those who waited in the upper room.

Ἐπιούσιον (epiousion) is not ordinary. It's not simply what we need to survive. It's what we need to be transformed.

It is substance + descent. Being + breath. Essence + Spirit.

It is God's own fullness, given not just to uphold us—but to dwell upon us, to become part of us, so that we are no longer merely living, but becoming.

What They Would Have Heard: Bread, Memory, Mystery

To those who first heard Jesus say this prayer, bread was never just bread.

Bread was survival. Bread was Torah. Bread was memory—of manna in the morning, of trust in the wilderness, of a God who gave just enough, just in time.

And so, as they listened:

"Give us today our ἐπιούσιον (epiousion) bread…"

The word struck them as strange.

They knew how to pray for bread. Daily bread. Manna bread. Sabbath bread.

But this was different. This word—ἐπιούσιον (epiousion)—wasn't part of their everyday language.

It would have sparked wonder, maybe confusion. Maybe even holy fear.

What did He just say? What kind of bread? Bread that comes upon essence? Bread that belongs to tomorrow? Bread from the heavens?

They may not have understood it then. Not fully.

But that's the nature of revelation.

It often arrives before it explains itself. Like manna—mysterious, unrepeatable, necessary.

A Prophetic Pause

And Jesus often spoke this way. Not to obscure the truth, but to plant it deep.

"You don't understand now," He told them, "but the Spirit will remind you..." (John 14:26)

This line in the Lord's Prayer was not just a petition. It was a prophetic seed.

They didn't know yet that it would be fulfilled in fire. That the ἐπιούσιον (epiousion) bread would one day come not only as provision—but as power. Not only as memory—but as mission.

But it began here. With a strange word. A shared hunger. And the first whisper of something coming.

Artos: The Bread That Became Him

The Greek word for bread here is ἄρτος (artos).

It's a simple word. Common. Familiar. Shared around tables in every village.

But in the mouth of Jesus, ἄρτος (artos) became something more.

"I am the Bread (ἄρτος - artos) of Life" (John 6:35).

He wasn't only comparing Himself to manna. He was naming Himself as the provision, the presence, the nourishment of essence and eternity.

When He took the bread at the table—He blessed it. He broke it. He gave it.

And He said: "This is My body…"

From that moment on, whenever they prayed "Give us today our daily bread," they weren't just asking for survival.

They were asking for Him.

The Bread Hidden in Three Measures

In Genesis 18, Sarah bakes three measures of flour for three mysterious visitors.

In the Gospels, Jesus speaks of a woman hiding leaven in three measures of flour—until it spreads through all of it.

At Pentecost, fifteen nations hear the Word at once.

Three measures. Hidden. Risen. Revealed.

This bread multiplies.

The pattern is ancient: what seems small, what appears hidden, what looks insufficient—becomes the place where heaven breaks through.

The ἐπιούσιον (epiousion) bread follows this same mystery. It comes not in abundance that overwhelms, but in measures that multiply through sharing, through trust, through the alchemy of community.

Not Scarcity. Abundance.

Manna could not be hoarded. But when gathered rightly, no one lacked.

The miracle was not just in falling from heaven, but in forming a people who trust enough to gather together.

Not consumers. Contributors.
Not survivors. Servants.
Not owners. Receivers.

This is the economics of the Kingdom—where ἐπιούσιον (epiousion) bread creates not competition but communion, not anxiety but abundance that flows from trust rather than accumulation.

The Bread is also the Word

Jesus says, "Man shall not live by bread alone, but by every word that proceeds from the mouth of God." (Matthew 4:4)

To pray for this Bread is to pray:

- Speak again.
- Breathe again.
- Form me again.

It is the prayer of new creation. It is Genesis remade.

The ἐπιούσιον (epiousion) bread is both sustenance and speech—the Word made flesh, the Logos becoming ἄρτος (artos), the divine essence taking form we can receive, digest, become.

Power and Presence

When Jesus stood before the Sanhedrin, He didn't defend Himself.

He said something they couldn't bear:

"From now on, the Son of Man will be seated at the right hand of the Power of God" (Luke 22:69).

The Power. He used it like a title. Not just as a name for God, but for the essence—the οὐσία (ousia) upon οὐσία (ousia)—the ἐπιούσια (epiousia).

The very place from which the Bread descends.

And then, after His resurrection and ascension, He vanished from sight.

But He didn't disappear. He ascended.

He sat down at the right hand of Power. And from there, He poured it out.

"You will receive power when the Holy Spirit comes upon you..." (Acts 1:8)

Power to witness. Power to heal. Power to gather and restore and become.

This is what they prayed for in the ἐπιούσιον (epiousion) line—though they didn't fully know it yet.

Not just bread for the day. But Power from on high.

Not just provision. But Presence that transforms.

Not just sustenance. But the Spirit of the risen Bread, given fresh each morning.

Luke's Spirit Whisper

Luke doesn't just give us a version of the Lord's Prayer. He gives us a whisper—a key, a clue, a Spirit-breathed hint.

Right after recording the prayer, he includes Jesus's words that seem to unlock the mystery behind the request for "daily bread":

"If you then, being evil, know how to give good gifts to your children, how much more will your heavenly Father give the Holy Spirit to those who ask Him?" (Luke 11:13)

Not bread. Not fish. The Spirit.

It's as if Luke leans in and says:

Do you see what this bread really is? Do you know what you're really asking for?

You are not just asking for food. You are asking for presence, for breath, for the power to live, to be, to witness.

You are asking for the Spirit who hovered in Genesis, who fell in Acts, who still comes—daily.

This whisper reframes the whole line.

"Give us today our daily bread…" becomes "Give us today the Spirit we cannot live without."

It is the same Word that said "Let there be light," now teaching us to say: "Let there be life in me."

Not just to eat. But to become.

The Fulfillment: Acts 2 and the Epiousion Harvest

What they prayed for with wonder, they received with fire.

Pentecost was not the birth of something new. It was the fulfillment of a prayer planted long before.

They had asked for bread—and heaven gave wind. They had opened their mouths in hunger—and the Spirit filled the house like breath into dust.

Tongues of fire appeared. Every nation heard. Hearts burned.

And the disciples? They received what Jesus had promised: Power.

The power to speak with boldness, to gather the scattered, to heal the broken, to love without fear, to witness without shame, to give without lack.

And they lived it daily.

They broke bread—ἄρτος (artos)—they devoted themselves to prayer, to one another, and to the Spirit who now rested upon them like the cloud had rested upon the tabernacle.

This was the daily bread. This was the ἐπιούσιον (epiousion). Not abstract. Not poetic. Real. Present. Transforming.

The prayer had become the pattern of their life.

And the Bread had become the Body. And the Body had become the Church. And the Spirit had made them one.

Sacred Space: Fed to Feed

This line is not about getting what we want. It's about being sustained to walk in what He gives.

To be fed so we can feed.

To be nourished so we can nurture.

To be formed so we can become living bread for a hungry world.

The ἐπιούσιον (epiousion) bread creates not consumers but contributors, not recipients but rivers, not the fed but the feeding.

When we receive this bread—this essence upon essence, this Spirit-breath, this daily descent of divine presence—we become what we receive.

We become bread broken and given.

We become presence poured out.

We become the answer to someone else's prayer for daily bread.

Ask today. Wait today. Receive today.

And let the Bread shape your becoming.

The Two Gifts That Form Us

Bread and Forgiveness

Before the prayer cries out for deliverance,
it settles into a quieter rhythm—
a rhythm of gift.

Two sacred offerings:
Bread.
Forgiveness.

This is not a shift in tone.
It is a descent into grace.

The first three lines oriented us upward—
toward the heavens, the name, the will.
We called out: Let be.
Let it be hallowed.
Let it come.
Let it be done.

Now, the prayer comes to us.
Into our hands.
Into our breath.

Gift One: Bread

This is not ordinary bread.
It is ἐπιούσιον (epiousion)—a word unlike any other.
Found nowhere else in ancient Greek.
Its meaning: super-essential.
Essence upon essence. Bread of being.

It is not just sustenance.
It is the Spirit's descent—
the presence of God becoming food,
life, power, mystery.

This bread nourishes more than the body.
It feeds faith.
It strengthens presence.
It prepares the soul to become dwelling space.

Daily it is offered.
Daily we ask.
Daily we are formed.

Gift Two: Forgiveness

This is not a contract.
It is a cleansing.

It is not just release from debt—
it is the breath that helps us see the door
we've been too afraid, ashamed, or weary to open.

And yet He draws us.
He does not force, but invites.
He does not demand, but offers.

We cannot open the door alone.
But we are not alone.
The One who knocks also strengthens the hand that opens.

Forgiveness is the Spirit's presence
breathing through shame,
through regret,
through tangled memory.

It is the unbinding of heart and mind.

To forgive is not to forget.
It is to remember rightly.
To see clearly.
To walk freely.

Yet forgiveness is not always easy.
It can feel like a blocked river,
a flow dammed by pain and fear.

In these moments, we discover
the deeper mystery:
that in seeing the other truly,
we begin to see ourselves.

In recognizing their woundedness,
we touch our own.

"Me in you and you in me"—
this sacred recognition
transforms forgiveness from duty to discovery,
from burden to liberation.

These are the two great gifts
that form the soul before the storm.

Bread for strength.
Forgiveness for freedom.

One empowers.
One unbinds.

And both are daily.
Both are divine.

They do not come from within us.
They come to us—
so that something may be born through us.

And all of it leads to the next cry:
Lead us… Deliver us…

Because now we are fed.
Now we are free.

Now—being fed and freed—
go feed and free others.

CHAPTER SIX

Forgive Us Our Debts, as We Forgive Our Debtors

καὶ ἄφες ἡμῖν τὰ ὀφειλήματα ἡμῶν, ὡς καὶ ἡμεῖς ἀφήκαμεν τοῖς ὀφειλέταις ἡμῶν (kai aphes hēmin ta opheilēmata hēmōn, hōs kai hēmeis aphēkamen tois opheiletais hēmōn)

Some prayers ask for bread.
This one asks for release.

There is a moment in the soul—
not when it is hungry,
but when it is heavy—
weighted with what it cannot repay.

The breath is caught.
The heart holds back.
Because guilt has a gravity of its own.

And then comes this line—
a quiet revolution in a single sentence:

Forgive us… as we forgive.
It does not plead.
It does not defend.
It opens.

It opens the hands that have clenched for too long.
It opens the soul to a flow that moves in two directions at once:
Receive. Release.
Be forgiven. Forgive.

Greek Word Study

καὶ ἄφες ἡμῖν τὰ ὀφειλήματα ἡμῶν,
ὡς καὶ ἡμεῖς ἀφήκαμεν τοῖς ὀφειλέταις ἡμῶν

ὀφειλήματα (opheilēmata) - "Debts"
This is the plural form of ὀφείλημα (opheilēma), from ὀφείλω
(opheilō), meaning:

- to owe, to be bound
- to be under obligation
- to be morally indebted

This isn't just financial. It's relational, moral, spiritual.
An unpayable debt. A shadow over the soul.

ἄφες (aphes) - "Forgive / Release"

- to let go
- to send away
- to release
- to remit

To forgive is to unbind. To set free.

ἀφήκαμεν (aphēkamen) - "We have forgiven"
Not future. Aorist active.
It assumes we've already begun to let go.

Forgiveness is not a transaction.
It is transformation. A holy motion in two directions.

Cultural & Theological Background

To Jesus's audience, forgiveness wasn't abstract—it was survival.
They knew debt in every form: economic, spiritual, social.
And they knew the promise of Jubilee:

a year when all debts would be released,
and all captives set free.

To pray this was to pray Jubilee.
To pray release.

And Jesus didn't only say it—He lived it.
He forgave sins out loud.
He scandalized the righteous.
And when they questioned His authority, He said:

> But so that you may know that the Son of Man has authority on
> earth to forgive sins… (Matthew 9:6)

And then He told the man to walk.

When Healing Begins in the Soul

Jesus looked at the paralyzed man and saw what no one else could:
a soul bound by shame.

Before He healed the body, He released the heart.

> Take heart, son; your sins are forgiven.

And suddenly—Shalom.
A wholeness that rose before the man did.

This is what forgiveness does.
It restores. Integrates. Makes whole.
The paralysis of the soul is lifted,
and the body follows.

The Flow of Grace

Forgiveness and release are the same river.
Grace received is grace released.
Mercy inhaled becomes mercy exhaled.
There is no holding one without letting go of the other.

Jesus made this visible in story after story.
He forgave debtors, welcomed prodigals, silenced accusers with mercy.

Forgiveness breaks the cycle.
It stops the spinning wheel of vengeance and shame.
Only the forgiven can forgive fully.
And we are all among them.

The Cross and the Divine Receipt: The Cleansing Flow

Jesus did not only teach forgiveness.
He became it.

> Father, forgive them… (Luke 23:34)

And from His side flowed blood and water.
Justice and mercy.
The price and the promise.

He bore our debts, not with clenched fists, but open arms.
He held the handwritten record—our χειρόγραφον (cheirographon)—
and nailed it to the cross.

And then He said:

It is finished.

τετέλεσται (tetelestai) - "Paid in full. Completed. Fulfilled forever."

Paul wrote it this way:

> He forgave us all our trespasses, canceling the record of debt…
> This He set aside, nailing it to the cross. (Colossians 2:13–14)

In Greek: χειρόγραφον (cheirographon)—our IOU, erased.
Stamped by heaven: τετέλεσται (tetelestai).
Not just forgiven—freed.
And the freedom remains.

The Challenge of the Flow

Yet we know this river sometimes feels dammed.
The flow restricted, blocked, diverted.
Some wounds cut deeper than words can reach.
Some debts feel too great to release.
Some shame too heavy to set down.

This struggle is part of the human journey,
and it does not diminish the call to forgive
or the power of grace.

Rather, it reminds us that forgiveness
is not a simple transaction but a profound transformation—
one that may happen in layers, in time, in tears.

From Calculation to Character: Peter's Question

"Lord, how many times shall I forgive my brother who sins against me? Up to seven times?" (Matthew 18:21)

Peter's question reveals the human instinct—
to measure, calculate, and limit forgiveness.
To make it a transaction rather than a transformation.

He seeks a formula.
A boundary.
A point where enough becomes enough.

But Jesus's answer shatters the entire premise:

"Not seven times, but seventy times seven" (Matthew 18:22).

This was not just a larger number.
It was an echo of ancient words—
Lamech's boast of seventy-sevenfold vengeance (Genesis 4:24).

Where Lamech's instinct was immediate, explosive revenge,
Jesus calls for immediate, unbounded forgiveness.

The problem wasn't Peter's number being too small.
The problem was that he was counting at all.

Jesus invites Peter not to do more,
but to become different.
To make forgiveness not a decision,
but a reflex.
Not a calculation,
but a character.

This is the journey from thinking like humans
to living as children of the Father.

Freedom, Not License

To forgive seventy times seven is not to erase all boundaries.
It is not to say, "Harm me again."
It is to say, "You cannot harm my soul."

Forgiveness frees the forgiver first.
It breaks chains that bind from within,
even when wisdom requires distance.

Jesus taught forgiveness without limits,
but also spoke of shaking dust from feet,
of discerning pearls before swine,
of being "wise as serpents, innocent as doves."

The river of grace flows internally
even when external boundaries must stand firm.

We can release the debt
without returning to the debtor's door.
We forgive not to enable,
but to be enabled—
to move forward unburdened,
to live unchained by another's actions.

This is the paradox:
We can love from a distance.
We can forgive while protecting.
We can release without returning.

The Gaze That Heals: Seeing Beyond Offense

Between enabling and abandoning
lies the third way of Jesus—
the way of seeing truly.

41

"Do you want to be made whole?" (John 5:6)

He asks the man by Bethesda's pool.
Not all wounds are ready for healing.
Not all who harm understand their chains.

But Jesus never averted His gaze.
He looked intently.
He saw beneath.
He discerned the readiness for transformation.

To forgive seventy times seven is not to blind ourselves,
but to see more clearly—
to recognize the bound ones who bind others,
to understand that hurting people hurt people.

True forgiveness neither enables harm
nor withdraws into safe distance.
It is the courage to stay present,
to look directly,
to keep seeing the divine image
beneath the distorted reflection.

Sometimes this means boundaries.
Sometimes it means engagement.
Always it means clarity of vision.

Love does not pretend.
It perceives.
It protects while it persists.

This is the mystery:
Forgiveness is never naive.
It is the most clear-eyed vision of all.

Forgiven Already: The Mystery of the Cross

"Father, forgive them, for they know not what they do" (Luke 23:34).

These words, spoken from the cross,
changed everything.

Not a conditional offer.
Not a future possibility.
A present reality.

The debt was canceled.
The price was paid.
The forgiveness accomplished—
whether received or not.

Here lies the great paradox:
Some continue paying debts
that no longer exist.
Some carry burdens
already lifted.

Like the servant in Jesus's parable,
forgiven an impossible sum,
who could not see himself as free—
and so imprisoned others and himself.

To forgive as we have been forgiven
is to recognize this truth:
The forgiveness is complete,
even when its reception is not.

We extend what has already been extended.
We release what has already been released.
We declare what has already been declared.

Some will walk away still bound,
choosing their chains over freedom.
This is not the failure of forgiveness,
but the mystery of human freedom.

Our role is not to force acceptance,
but to maintain the open door,
the extended hand,
the clear-eyed gaze that says:

"It is finished.
Whether you know it yet or not,
whether you live in it yet or not,
the debt is paid."

Seeing Clearly, Forgiving Completely

"Father, forgive them, for they know not what they do."
Complete. Universal. Without reservation.

"Do you want to be made whole?"
Discerning. Personal. Requiring response.

Both are Jesus.
Both are true.

This is the sacred balance:
The debt is fully canceled at the cross—
a cosmic forgiveness that encompasses all.
Yet relationship remains a dance of two freedoms.

To see clearly is not to withhold forgiveness—
it is to understand how to express it wisely.
To forgive completely is not to abandon discernment—
it is to ensure our boundaries come from love, not vengeance.

Jesus forgave everyone from the cross,
yet He did not entrust Himself to everyone.
He knew what was in each person.
He discerned where transformation was welcome.

This is our calling too—
to hold the universal forgiveness as accomplished reality,
while exercising wisdom in how we embody it relationally.

We forgive because it is already done.
We discern because love requires wisdom.

The forgiving heart sees clearly without condemning.
The discerning mind loves fully without enabling.

This is the miraculous integration—
to be wise as serpents, innocent as doves,
to forgive without limit while loving with wisdom.

The Bound Cannot Unbind

When we stand before others with judgment still burning,
we reveal not their chains, but our own.

The log in our own eye is not just pride or hypocrisy—
it is often the weight of self-condemnation,
the burden of guilt we refuse to release.

And from that shadow place,
we cannot truly see another's need for grace.

The miracle happens when we first receive:
"You are forgiven."

When we allow those words to sink deeper than our shame,
to touch the places we've declared unredeemable.

Then—only then—can our hands truly open.

The forgiven forgive not from obligation,
but from revelation.
From the wonder of discovering:
What has been healed in me can now heal others.

The Sacred Mirror: Seeing and Being Seen

Perhaps the deepest mystery of forgiveness is this:
When we truly see the other, we begin to see ourselves.
When we recognize our own humanity in another's failure,
our own fragility in another's woundedness,
something transformative happens.

We are not forgiving a stranger, but a reflection.
Not an enemy, but another self.

This is the radical vision Jesus offers—
not just that we should forgive,
but that in forgiving, we discover our shared being.

       Me in you and you in me.

When this recognition dawns,
forgiveness is no longer just duty or command.
It becomes the natural movement of wholeness
recognizing itself across the divide.

And in that recognition, both are freed.

Sacred Space: Set Free, To Set Free

We all know what it feels like to carry regret.
To replay the moment.
To feel the weight of what we wish we could undo.

And sometimes—more often than we realize—
the person we struggle most to forgive
is ourselves.

This line in the Lord's Prayer is not just about releasing others.
It is about being released, fully.
Even from ourselves.

> Forgive us… as we forgive.

Not two actions. One motion.
Inhale. Exhale.
Grace in. Grace out.

You are forgiven.
You are free.

And in that freedom,
you are given authority to walk into places where others are still bound
and whisper what was once whispered to you:

> You are no longer held by what held you.

"You can rise."

To forgive is to release.
To release is to bless.
To bless is to become like the One who first forgave you.

> The blood says: You are forgiven.
> The water says: You are alive.

And the voice of the Son says:

> It is finished.

Now go, and bring freedom.

CHAPTER SEVEN

Lead Us Not Into Testing, But Deliver Us From the Evil One

καὶ μὴ εἰσενέγκῃς ἡμᾶς εἰς πειρασμόν, ἀλλὰ ῥῦσαι ἡμᾶς ἀπὸ τοῦ πονηροῦ
(kai mē eisenenkēs hēmas eis peirasmon, alla rhysai hēmas apo tou ponērou)

The Sifting and the Prayer

Simon, Simon…
The voice is not harsh,
but it carries thunder beneath the calm.
Twice He says his name—
as if to pull Peter back from the edge of a moment he cannot yet see.

"Satan has asked to sift you like wheat."

The word carries weight.
Ἐξητήσατο (exētēsato).
Not just asked—demanded.
Like a prosecutor claiming a right.
But he has no right.
He needs permission.

Even now, the darkness must knock.
Even now, it must bow before the throne of mercy.

The evil one does not reign.
He is still restrained.
This is not the hour of his rule—only of his allowance.

And Jesus does not stop it.
He doesn't say "I blocked him."
He says something far more profound:

"But I have prayed for you…"

Already.
Before the shadow comes, the prayer has gone before.
Before the shaking begins, the voice of the Son
has spoken your name in eternity.

This is not abandonment.
It is a witness in the whirlwind.
A presence in the pressure.
A Word in the wilderness.

"That your faith may not fail."
Not if.
When.
Not maybe.
But when you have turned back,
strengthen your brothers.

He doesn't just pray against the trial.
He speaks through it.
Beyond it.
He sees Peter already returning.
Already restored.
Already reaching back to pull others from the sifting.

This is deliverance before the descent.
This is the mercy that eclipses the accuser.
And it mirrors a line long spoken before:

"Lead us not into testing,
but deliver us from the evil one…"

The Words That Carry the Cry

This line of the prayer is not resignation.
It is not fear.
It is not pleading for ease.
It is the voice of the child
calling to the Father who watches through the storm
and walks on water.

It begins with a request:

εἰσενέγκῃς (eisenenkēs)
"Do not bring us in…"

Not a fearful command, but a faithful plea.
A single, decisive act:

"Do not let us enter a testing that swallows."

It is not avoidance.
It is trust.

Then comes the weight:

πειρασμόν (peirasmon)
"Testing. Trial. Proving."

Not enticement to evil.
God tempts no one with wickedness.
This is the fire that refines,
not the bait that deceives.
It's the wind against the ship
that proves the shape of its sails.

The trial is not the enemy.
The lie it whispers is.

So the prayer shifts:

ῥῦσαι ἡμᾶς (rhysai hēmas)
"Rescue us.
Deliver us."

This is no gentle suggestion.
It's the cry of one who knows the grip of water.

"Pull us from the drag of distortion."
"Take hold of us, not later—but now."

And from what?

ἀπὸ τοῦ πονηροῦ (apo tou ponērou)
"From the evil one."

Not the idea of evil.
Not the abstraction.
But the voice that accuses.
The shadow that mimics.
The devourer who seeks whom he may.

We pray this not to escape reality,
but to live awake inside of it—
to know the truth,
and not be undone by the storm's lie.

This prayer is not bargaining.
It's belonging.
It's knowing who to cry to—
and knowing He comes when we call.

Rendered with Spirit and Sense

(A full-verse poetic translation)

καὶ μὴ εἰσενέγκῃς ἡμᾶς εἰς πειρασμόν,

And do not bring us into the trial—
not as judgment, not as abandonment,
but preserve us from entering what might undo.

ἀλλὰ ῥῦσαι ἡμᾶς ἀπὸ τοῦ πονηροῦ.

But draw us out—deliver us—
from the evil one who distorts and devours.

This is no bargain. It is a trust cry.
A single call to the Rescuer who sees, comes, and saves.

The Wind That Lies and the Breath That Stands

Peter stepped out into what he thought was wind.
He felt it rushing—violent, swirling, tearing at him.
But the deeper truth was harder to name.

It was resistance.
Not just of nature,
but of spirit.

The word in Greek is ἄνεμος (anemos)—the storm-wind.
The kind that lashes and howls without form.
The kind that breaks things, not builds them.

But it is not the same word
as the breath that hovered over the deep.
Not the same as the wind that filled the upper room.
Not the whisper in the garden.
Not the breath in the lungs of clay.

That wind—πνεῦμα (pneuma)—is holy.
It gives. It fills. It births.
And it does not move with chaos.

It moves with harmony.
With unity.
With flow.

Like birds in flight that turn as one.
Like fish in deep waters
that shimmer and twist without collision.

Πνεῦμα (pneuma) orchestrates.
It guides.
It forms and inhabits.
It brings life.

But ἄνεμος (anemos) rips.
It spins without center.
It mimics the breath,
but only to deceive.

Peter saw it—and feared.
He turned his eyes from the "Come."
He began to sink.

This is the enemy's tactic—
not always to crush,
but to distract.

To obscure the light,
and then whisper that it's gone.

But the wind is a lie.
And the storm is not sovereign.
And the One who walks on water
is still walking.

Exposing the Lie, Revealing the Truth

There is a lie in the storm. It doesn't shout. It whispers…
You're not loved. You're not seen. This is your fault.
But the lie proves the truth it tries to hide. If there were no truth, there
would be no lie.

The testing is not the danger. The unseen God is not absent. The trial is
not to destroy, but to reveal:

You are seen. You are being strengthened. You are not alone.
A bridge builder tests to prove strength, not to expose weakness. And
what God allows, He has already entered.

When He Watches from the Mountain

They rowed for hours. Against the wind. Against their strength.
Against what they could not name.
And they thought they were alone. But He had never stopped watching.
The Greek says it plainly: βασανιζομένους (basanizomenous)—
straining, tormented, tested. Their effort was painful. The sea was
resisting them.

But Jesus was on the mountain. And He was praying.
And He saw them. Not vaguely. Not from a distance. He saw them
with intent. With knowing. With love.

He watched as a parent watches a child learning to walk through trembling. He did not come immediately—not because He delayed, but because He trusted.

He waited, not to punish, but to reveal. And then—He came.

Not rushed. Not panicked. But walking. On the very thing they feared.

"He intended to pass by them…" (Mark 6:48)

But this was not a bypass. It was a revelation.

This phrase echoes an older mountain. Another storm. Another cleft.

"I will cause all My goodness to pass before you…" (Exodus 33:19)

Moses hid in the cleft of the rock. The disciples strained in the cleft of the storm.

In both, glory passed by. But only in one did it stay.

Moses was spoken to as a friend speaks to a friend—face to face in intimacy and awe—but still, the fullness could not be seen.

"You cannot see my face, for no one may see me and live…" (Exodus 33:20)

But now, on Galilee's waters, the I AM does not just pass by.

He is beheld. He is received. He speaks. He steps in.

And John would later write:

"We beheld His glory…" (John 1:14)

Not just a glimpse. The fullness. Grace and truth in the flesh.

The disciples do not just survive the storm. They worship in the boat.

"Truly, You are the Son of God." (Matthew 14:33)

The cleft of the rock becomes the quiet place in the wind-stilled boat.

The hidden face becomes the face that saves.

He does not vanish into the storm. He remains.

CHAPTER EIGHT

For Yours Is the Kingdom, and the Power, and the Glory, Forever. Amen.

ὅτι σοῦ ἐστιν ἡ βασιλεία καὶ ἡ δύναμις καὶ ἡ δόξα εἰς τοὺς αἰῶνας· ἀμήν
(hoti sou estin hē basileia kai hē dynamis kai hē doxa eis tous aiōnas; amēn)

The Echo That Seals the Prayer

It was not in the earliest manuscripts. Not in Matthew's original ending. Not in Luke's shorter version of the prayer. The ancient scrolls leave this final line unstated.

And yet—it was always in the heart of the Church.

A whispered crescendo. A rising benediction. A doxology that grew from worship, not from scribal addition, but from Spirit-filled awe.

"For Yours is the kingdom, and the power, and the glory, forever. Amen."

It echoes the ancient prayer of David—when the ark was brought near and the people gave freely:

"Yours, O Lord, is the greatness, and the power, and the glory, and the victory, and the majesty... Yours is the kingdom, O Lord" (1 Chronicles 29:11).

Though likely added later by Byzantine worshipers, this final doxology feels deeply aligned with the voice of Matthew—the Gospel writer who saw in Jesus the long-awaited King. If not his pen, it carries his heartbeat. The Kingdom. The power. The glory. All His. Forever.

This language fits the Church Matthew wrote for—a people shaped by longing for the Messiah, for the throne of David, for a kingdom that could never be shaken.

And among the earliest to speak life in Antioch was Barnabas—a man whose very name means "Son of Encouragement" or "Son of Prophetic Consolation." He did not just preach the kingdom—he carried it in his voice. And alongside Paul, he formed the language of a Church that learned to say:

"Yours is the kingdom, and the power, and the glory…"

The Church was still learning. Still becoming. And as the Spirit moved, so did their understanding. It makes sense that these words would rise. Not as revision, but as revelation.

Paul spoke of psalms and hymns and spiritual songs, because the Church was being taught to sing as she was taught to pray.

The doxology reflects that—the rising praise of a people who had seen the storm stilled, who had tasted the bread, who had felt the chains fall, and now, in awe, could only say:

"All of it is Yours."

The Kingdom

σοῦ ἐστιν ἡ βασιλεία (sou estin hē basileia) - "Yours is the kingdom…"

The prayer began with kingdom. Let it come. Let it reign. Let it be done.

But now, at the close, we are not asking. We are acknowledging.

It is not a kingdom to be won. It is already Yours. Always has been. Always will be.

This is the kingdom not of grasping power, but of open hands. The kingdom of mustard seeds, of hidden treasure, of banquet tables spread for the unlikely.

It is not built by human conquest but by surrendered hearts.

It is not established with warhorses, but with water basins and towels. It spreads not through domination, but incarnation.

To say "Yours is the kingdom" is to lay down every counterfeit crown, every empire built of fear, and say:

Only You reign rightly.

The Power

καὶ ἡ δύναμις (kai hē dynamis) - "And the power…"

Not force. Not coercion. But δύναμις (dynamis)—the word that echoes in Acts 1:8:

"You will receive power when the Holy Spirit comes upon you…"

This is creative power—the kind that speaks light into darkness. Healing power—that restores what others would discard. Resurrecting power—that calls what was dead to live again.

And it is Yours. Always Yours. And You do not hoard it. You share it with sons and daughters.

Power to forgive. Power to walk free. Power to bless those who curse. Power to speak and silence storms.

Your power is not a threat. It is a promise.

The Glory

καὶ ἡ δόξα (kai hē doxa) - "And the glory…"

Not the spotlight. Not the applause.

Glory—δόξα (doxa)—is weight. The radiance of essence. The fullness of being revealed.

It is what Moses could only glimpse. It is what the disciples beheld in the storm. It is what now fills the hearts of those who've been fed and freed.

The glory of God is not just light—it is recognition. When the soul sees and knows: This is who He is. This is what I was made for.

The glory is Yours, and You do not hide it. You veil it just long enough for us to survive it, and then You invite us in.

Glory that becomes communion. Glory that becomes transformation. Glory that becomes our own reflection—not because we are great, but because we are Yours.

The Amen

ἀμήν (amēn) - "Amen."

It is not a period. It is not the end. It is not the closing of eyes or the folding of hands.

It is a doorway. A signature. A seal.

Ἀμήν (amēn) means: Let it be. Not just "I agree," but I align.

Let it be so in heaven. Let it be so on earth. Let it be so in me.

This Ἀμήν (amēn) is not whispered in fear—it is spoken in faith.

It is the echo of the first three: Let it be hallowed. Let it come. Let it be done.

60

It is the breath of the middle two: Feed us. Forgive us.

It is the cry of the final one: Rescue us.

And now it becomes our word. Not just the prayer Jesus taught, but the life He formed in us.

This is the Ἀμήν (amēn) that stands on storm-stilled seas, that rises with resurrection breath, that dares to say—

"You are the kingdom." "You are the power." "You are the glory." "You are my Ἀμήν (amēn)."

Revelation Rising

The doxology may not have begun as part of the prayer, but it feels born from it—as if the disciples, slowly awakening to the δύναμις (dynamis) and the δόξα (doxa)—the power and the glory—found themselves unable to end with anything but awe.

This is the moment when prayer shifts: from recitation to recognition, from petition to praise, from request to revelation.

They understood the weight of what they held. And they responded the only way they could:

Yours. All of it. Forever.

Sacred Space: A Throne Within

What if this prayer was never meant to end?

What if "Ἀμήν (amēn)" wasn't the closing of the prayer, but the opening of our life?

The words have ascended: from heaven's name to earth's hunger, from the cry for rescue to the coronation of the King.

And now—they rest.

But only for a moment.

Because now, you carry the throne inside you.

Not the weight of responsibility—but the mystery of presence.

"Yours is the kingdom…" Then let that kingdom rule in me. Let it soften the clenched places, reorder the loud rooms, quiet the tyrants of fear and shame.

"Yours is the power…" Then let me walk not by might, not by pretending to be strong, but by Your breath in my bones. Let weakness become the doorway of wonder.

"Yours is the glory…" Then let me live radiant, not for praise, but because I've seen You. And I am changed.

This is the sacred paradox: The throne is eternal, but its echo is intimate.

He rules the cosmos, but whispers your name. He calms the sea, but enters your silence.

And so you sit now—not as a servant fearing the scepter, but as a child loved by the King.

The kingdom is not far.
The power is not delayed.
The glory is not dim.
It is here.
It is now.
And it is Yours to walk in.

Selah

Complete Scripture Index

Bibliography

Primary Sources

Greek Old Testament (Septuagint)

- Rahlfs, Alfred, and Robert Hanhart, eds. Septuaginta: Vetus Testamentum Graecum. Göttingen: Vandenhoeck & Ruprecht, 1931-.

Greek New Testament

- Nestle-Aland, Novum Testamentum Graece. 28th ed. Stuttgart: Deutsche Bibelgesellschaft, 2012.

Lexical Resources

Greek Lexicons

- Bauer, Walter, Frederick W. Danker, William F. Arndt, and F. Wilbur Gingrich. A Greek-English Lexicon of the New Testament and Other Early Christian Literature. 3rd ed. Chicago: University of Chicago Press, 2000.

This work emerges from direct engagement with the original Greek text, seeking to hear these words as Jesus's first audience would have heard them, unfiltered by centuries of interpretation

www.ingramcontent.com/pod-product-compliance
Lightning Source LLC
LaVergne TN
LVHW041326080426
835513LV00008B/606